LEAVING THE RELIGION OF SELF-HARM

BAILEY BLUMENSTOCK

Leaving the Religion of Self-Harm
© Bailey Blumenstock / Cathexis Northwest Press

No part of this book may be reproduced without written permission
of the publisher or author, except in reviews and articles.

First Printing: 2025

ISBN: 978-1-952869-93-8

Editing & Design by C. M. Tollefson
Cathexis Northwest Press

cathexisnorthwestpress.com

LEAVING THE RELIGION OF SELF-HARM

BAILEY BLUMENSTOCK

Cathexis Northwest Press

The brilliant premise of Bailey Blumenstock's gorgeous debut, *Leaving the Religion of Self-Harm*, is that all ways of life—that is, all the ways we have grooved our minds into patterns of behavior—are a kind of religion. Some link us into our higher nature, our better selves; others begin in Hell like Dante had to and travel upward with the help of a guide. Blumenstock's guide is poetry itself (as it was for Dante, whose persona was enfolded into Virgil), and her Mary figure at the peak of Paradise is Leonardo's Ginevra de Benci, to whom a staggering invocation opens this book. Following the poet's progress, we discover that the first impulse toward the new religion of self-endearment is merely to apprehend, to simply *hear* the care that is felt for us by others. At the beginning of these changes, the Ginevra floats at great distance, like many of the objects and animals encountered throughout the book. By the end of the collection, we have become her: and it is we who look back upon the other goddess, the suicide at the bottom of the Seine, in the devastating final portrait, hearing *her* with our newfound compassion for the world. I have never read a short volume of poetry so complete in its transubstantiation of earthly bread into the body of Christ. This is a profound achievement from a poet whose work in letters has only begun.

— David Keplinger, author of *Ice*

There are few poetic voices who can whisper and scream in turn and pull them each off with equal strength, but Bailey Blumenstock holds these—and many more contradictions—beside each other with tremendous skill. We encounter both the robins with matching blouses and the quiet horror of the unjustly hung elephant. There's the looming desire to die and yet the vision of splendor and gentleness still to come. And here: The slanted holiness of a backyard exorcism trailed by the National Cathedral. Among all of these seemingly contrasting moments is a deep yearning to escape the current moment: through contemplations of the past, considerations of a future without so much pain, pleading for an answer to the ever-present prayer, "God help." *Leaving the Religion of Self-Harm* is a staggeringly strong debut collection demonstrating Blumenstock's dazzling breadth of references, generosity of imagery, and declaration of that which is holy simply by being named as such.

— Jordan Pérez, author of *Santa Tarantula*

To live—to live within our minds—is to know life is both lush and treacherous. The fool forgets the latter, and the pessimist forgets the former. Bailey Blumenstock's *Leaving the Religion of Self-Harm* is a brave book that sings from that uncertain space between those poles of luxuriance and peril—full of many days when we may not want to wake, and many where we could not imagine not meeting the sun again. We witness Blumenstock finding a new "religion," a new faith filtered through lyrical concision and candor. If there is a reason we read poems, it is to see—in that brevity, that prayer, of a small page—that there are others reaching for belief, just like us.

— Kyle Dargan, author of *Anagnorisis*

For Mr. Porter

Table of Contents

Benedictions before the Ginevra de Benci	1
The Ark on Mt. Ararat	2
On the Recovery of Sputnik II, 1957	3
մայրիկ	4
Commute	5
Cathedral	6
Leaving the Religion of Self-Harm	7
North America Nebula	9
Creation Myth	10
Portrait of the Dissociated Personality as Quinta Del Sordo	11
Jellyfish	12
President Biden Recognizes the Armenian Genocide, April 2022	13
Migraine	14
Elephant	15
When the Space Shuttle *Columbia* Exploded Over Texas	16
First Date	17
Matthew 6:28	18
Craighill Channel Lower Range Front Lighthouse	19
The Other Pandemic	20
Isaiah 3:24	21
Vision	22
Self-Portrait as Unknown Woman of the Seine	23

Benedictions before the Ginevra de Benci

May your legs not buckle before her.
May you resist the temptation to lay down your coat and sleep.
May the guard pity you, not knowing why.
May you go otherwise unnoticed.

May you carry a toothbrush in your purse.
May you remember your pills and to take them
May you brush your hair before you go.
May you eat again.

Blessed be the skull that cages the thrashing brain.
Blessed be the cavity around the thrashing heart.
Sadness raises its fist in your throat.
Your fingers tremble as the breaking begins.
In your place her gaze meets a child

May you tend to your broken heart.
May you sleep through the night.
May she weep for you.
May you hear.

The Ark on Mt. Ararat

Some say it is only a shadow of a rock on a rock,
or a smear of holy ink, or a bruise, or a cross of volcanic ash
on the forehead of the cliff face. The last person
in my family who saw the Mountain disappeared.
Her daughter came to America to marry a jeweler. There is nothing
left of us but rings: one on my mother's left hand, dozens buried
in a graveyard outside of Philadelphia
on the ring fingers of unmarried women who kept convent
at a house on Spring Garden street, another
in a casket next to a parking lot, tucked in my grandmother's fist.
Sit on a hospital bed, dying, in University City.
See a spire out the window. This is the church
where my grandmother prayed as a child, kneeling in the bluish
light of a stained-glass mountain. From the back pew,
see the ship rocking on the gravel tongue.

On the Recovery of Sputnik II, 1957

Before the launch,
the mission scientist bathed her,
dabbed her with alcohol and bruises of iodine.
He kissed her nose.
She had played with his children.
In photographs, the hatch is open and she is posed,
or is posing, one ear folded, the other heavenward.
At launch, the saucer-sized porthole fogged with her panting.
For one hundred and sixty-three days after my father's
thirteenth birthday, her corpse circled the earth.
By the $2,570^{th}$ orbit, my mother
had toddled for the first time,
the dog's skeleton ship winking from above.
Zhuchka, little bug, so far from Moscow. *Limonchik*,
chained to a satellite, a blip in the firmament.
Kudryavka, little curl, the mongrel cosmonaut.
Laika, they called her, *dog*.

մայրիկ[1]

I pull nests of black hair   from my mouth   in the shower

momma   pulls the hair from the drain   wraps the strands

to her loom and weaves them   straight and soft   makes a

blanket   wraps my body in it   my fingers and toes

are broken   the tips angled over many gold rings

she sets them   with the veined leaves of an aloe plant

       my palms slip into hers   as she begs me

bailey,   do not try to crawl   back into my womb

your birth   nearly killed me   must you hold me

now   so tightly   like a gun?

---

[1] *Mother*

Commute

Trains arrive every seven minutes at rush hour
but it is best to do it at midday when they
come less frequently. This is also when
the passengers are most likely to be families
or college students, people you hope
have more sympathy than the commuting
businessmen who, you think, must not understand art
or sadness. You suppose that you do not either if
you are waiting in a metro station for your executioner
while wearing sneakers. The station fills and empties
over and over, and you are vaguely reminded of the ocean,
which, you think, could make a fine line
in a poem if you get out of here. The brief
notion of survival causes you to consider
the person currently driving the hurtling
metal truncheon out of Gallery Place and up
to Mt. Vernon Square, maybe thinking
of lunch, or of quitting his job, or just how much
he loves sitting in the front seat of the machine
you are going to ask to kill you. If only there were
some way you could ask him if it was okay
to jump in front of his train. Then you could
let him know that it is not his fault, it is yours,
that you are already kind of dead, actually,
to be considering dying. And really, if all
the bus drivers and cyclists of the city
could have just been a bit more reckless,
you probably could already be dead. So,
you'd tell him, blame them, not you,
for the inevitable mess. Somewhere now,
from inside of you, you recognize the sudden
wind and stink of rubber as his arrival.
The train rears his head through the tunnel, flashes
its mighty eyes, looks through you to the animal
cowering in the cave of your heart.

Cathedral

Looking at it now,
I can't remember which spire
she stole us away to
while the choir bleated
through the Magnificat
I do not know what it says about me
that I remember the carpeted elevator,
but not the view,
the fear of being caught,
but not the amazement,
the way my head ached,
but not her breath,
the yearning for God,
but not the glory

Leaving the Religion of Self-Harm

I board
the moored,
brooding ship,

still swaying
from the night before.
The apostates

take my things,
what is left of me,
cure my mouth

with salt water
to last a winter,
without mead,

drain my blood
for now I am
done bleeding.

The ship
heaves into
the Atlantic,

and I am
somehow alive
again

and uncertain
of what has
always been true:

is there really no purpose
for my body
other than hurt?

The wind changes
and after
days of night

light comes
again to
Jerusalem.

And then
the ship
slips through

the break
alights onto
strange sand.

Another
cathedral
waits for me.

North America Nebula

Spencer says, point it here, and I hold my phone
with two hands and aim it across the river,
to the deep blue lunula beyond the mountains.
The virtual map labels that emptiness the *North America Nebula*
and suddenly, I want to pray. Drunk,
I lay in the frozen leaves and say, *where we came forth*
and once more saw the stars drunk, my friends laugh,
drunk, someone stumbles, spills champagne into my hair
and two days later, my father will fall again.
In a place with no stars, I will go to church,
and tell no one.

Creation Myth

I remember so little of my life, but twenty years later
I remember laughing, laughing like praying,
laughing not at God, but with him.
We have Easter at the Aunts' house
516 S. 46th Street. I don't
remember my father being there,
so full the house was of women,
but he was, the only one passing on pilaf
and madzoon when it is given to him.
Yam isn't hayastana, Nana says,
both to him and around him,
but that's alright. He disappears
after dinner to the back stoop
to get high before the drive home
and while he is gone, Tecate sits
at the spinnet and plays hymns
from memory while her sisters sing.
Nana performs her tenor part—an affected warble—
and then we are all laughing.

Portrait of the Dissociated Personality as Quinta Del Sordo

after Francisco Goya's Black Paintings, painted on the walls of his house, and not intended for anyone but himself.

The ribcage is where you keep the laughing women, the reading men,
the men eating soup, the men fighting with cudgels,

the shadow playing the role of Holofernes cowering under Judith's knife
and the silver dish where his head will fall

the god devouring his son (the wild eating so familiar to you, one body
glutting itself on another), the witches' sabbath beneath the cruciform sternum,

dirty feet and faces mooning before a blackened tumor cloaked as Baphomet.

And behind the horned God, the Fates, and behind the Fates, pilgrims, clustered
like fish eggs, singing and praying as one mouth made of many little mouths

(and your mother plays a piccolo and your father plays a drum)
and above them all, suspended from the vaulted ceiling

the fantastic vision: the heart.

Jellyfish

Immortal jellyfish grow to 4.5 mm, the size of a rosary bead. The bell is perfectly transparent, disclosing the cruciate stomach to the sea, red and diffusive as menstrual blood. When held in a human palm, it appears only as a puncture, like something blunt was thrust into the skin and then removed again. If hurt or anxious, the jelly, brainless, shatters into a polyp, a colony of child-creatures, and each begins the process of growing up all over again. Unless eaten or captured, this reliving can go on forever, each new medusa squeezed into the ocean and left alone to drift. In a bathtub, on an island, one block from the sea, a father washes his daughter's hair. Salps and comb jellies fall from her into the grey water like drops of lead crystal fall from a chandelier: the child-creature breaking. The showerhead cries and cries. When the father is done, she is so small. She fits in his hand, mouth.

President Biden Recognizes the Armenian Genocide, April 2022

At West Laurel Hill cemetery
next to the Schuylkill expressway
we are buried under names
holy and chimeric
far from Antioch and Mt. Ararat and Kessab

but just a few miles from jeweler's row
where our father cut diamonds
and the Wanamaker's
and Northminster Presbyterian Church

our houses on Hamilton street and Spring Garden Street
and South 46th street rest now
for we are not ghosts

we do not haunt. Yet how
we miss each other.
Put your ear to the ground
and hear the word of genocide:

George, the easy white name our father chose
Here we are only as *Hayastana* as our tombstones:
no one remembers the language anymore

this is the Gospel of Diaspora

Migraine

        I must tell myself   the aura   is a host of
angels

Ophanim: dozens of eyes   orbiting close to
creation

         burning across   and beyond

                                                                       my vision
is it heresy   to imagine God

                 so small

surrounded by   beating   vulvas   of Seraphim?

is it heresy   to inject sumatriptan   into my thigh

                                                                  dissolving Him
and his fiery thrones?   if so, I say unto you

             genuflecting   over the toilet bowl

it is an heretic   *that makes the fire*

                                        not she which burns in it.[1]

---

[1] *The Winter's Tale (II.iii)*

Elephant

One great tooth was infected,
hollow as a gun barrel.
Before the parade, they gave her
bourbon to drink and capped
the tusk with brass, draped
a thin velvet cape over
the crumpled skin of her back,
strung beads from one
beaten ear to the other.
When the man mounted her
holding the bullhook aloft
like a knight before the joust,
she noticed only the smoothness
of the cobble beneath her,
the wide-eyed child, held high
on someone's shoulders,
the lilies the city planted
in anticipation of her arrival
And then the steel prod
met her cheek at the place
where the infected bone found flesh
and carved a canker there.
She screamed a sound hoarse
from submission and bucked,
the man pitched onto the street.
When her foot found his skull
and shattered it, she felt nothing
but the heat of the sun, unadorned
warm on her neck and pate,
perhaps knowing that tomorrow,
as she sways in the noose looped to the derrick,
she will only be able to look up.

When the Space Shuttle *Columbia* Exploded Over Texas

the newscaster used the word disintegrate—
to describe what was really a cluster
of many suns, or a supernova, or the pillars of creation untethered
hurtling towards the earth.
I was eight and from a TV in New Jersey
to me it was beautiful. I touched the TV screen
wiped away the static curtain, felt the electrodes scuttle on my open palm.
No one told me that I was watching
people die the worst deaths anyone alive has ever died
or that after the heat of re-entry
consciousnesses was impossible after the first minute.
After the second, heads yawed and fused into helmets,
after an hour, a torso careened into a forest.
I was eight and afraid to die,
But felt no fear as the sky on TV bloomed and crackled,
or as the newscaster, unflinching,
reported that a human heart was found
among the scattered and charred remains, whole.

First Date

You would not believe me if I told you
that my first date with J was an exorcism.
He said he'd never done one before

and he didn't want to hurt me. Secretly
I hoped it would hurt just a little
You would not believe me if I told you

that we went to a professional, a fundamentalist
who had set up shop in a brand new chapel, still shrink wrapped
She said, "I've never done this before—

"what did you say its name was?" She
laid her hands on my heart and they both began to pray
Would you believe me if I told you

that when I started to believe a little in my own salvation,
I heaved demonic jelly into a paper cup? Truthfully,
I had never done that before

When we got home, J consecrated chocolate milk and toast
we took communion, he held my hand
Believe me when I tell you,
I had never been loved like that before.

Matthew 6:28

When it becomes too much,
God gives me a palm of birdseed
and starlings on the grass outside the National Cathedral

Starlings in the trees picking bloody berries
and robins in their matching blouses
and one lonely bird with a blue tail

that I cannot name but I know you'd love
I sing to him: *For the true believer, everything is a sign* [1].
and he seems to cock his head as if to remind me

that the bigness of grief is equal to the depth of love lost
and how I loved you, baby, and how I love you still.

---

[1] *The Mountain Goats,* "*In the Shadow of the Western Hills.*"

Craighill Channel Lower Range Front Lighthouse

For Josh

wades in the Chesapeake somewhere near your parents' place. On my birthday, your dad takes us out in the boat and circles it, over and over, while the sun sets. The lighthouse, somehow, has a house number, a mailbox. The water is opalescent and strange. I think to ask you, *must all abandoned things be haunted?* I think to ask you, *must all things be filled to be whole?* I almost say, "Is this heaven?" and God catches the cliche on my tongue.

The Other Pandemic

For several Davids

I moved back into the city in June
relieved to be out of urban village limbo

out of unvaccinated, hysterical limbo
out of the apartment that looked over

a shallow swimming pool and a chain
coffee shop and a row of fast-casual

restaurants that never opened
No one in that building stayed for

very long. But let me tell you,
and this is true: one night as it rained

I stood outside at the feet of all
the high-rises and saw a rainbow

fluttering in the dark, an illusion
of drunkenness or a trick of the light

and then an old friend, someone from college,
a Dantean suicide, coming over the crest of the hill

walking in the middle of the empty intersection,
hands in the pockets of a brown leather jacket

slick with rain, as I remembered him.

Isaiah 3:24

I lie on the floor to talk to God
and the carpet smells like cat piss, which reminds me of despair,
because the olfactory bulb and the amygdala are in love.

It takes the epidermis one month to completely renew itself with stem cells, to rid itself of
every inch of skin you ever touched: the olfactory bulb and the amygdala are in love
and the skin that smelled like you is now dust

I lie on my face before God and ask Him if I should buy you lilies,
for you don't care much for clothes, nor labor
And when I smell coffee, I think of you and my father, arguing in the kitchen

then I think of your mother, driving us home with a broken arm.
I cut lemons in the back of the cafe and think of a Sunday evening,
doing the crossword over margaritas, when you told me you didn't love me
and then took it back,

and then think of a few Sundays later when you changed your mind again.
Beloved, I never hated you, even when you washed and neatly folded my clothes
before returning them to me.

I lie at the feet of God and search the carpet for strands of your thick, black hair.
The two-word prayer you taught me feels pointless now: *God help, God help, God help*
the olfactory bulb and the amygdala are in love, like we are not.

Vision

In some faraway port, somewhere fish-smelling
and full of whistling, working men
I'm picking barnacles the size of my heart.
There are little boats strung with bells and tied to the dock,
bobbing and ringing. It's somewhere blue
and European: rows and rows of townhouses
that look like my father's broken teeth.
I have no body but feel the sun, warm as a hand on my neck

and on the floor of my apartment
the crying-thing crawls from my throat,
and I sob, soaking the carpet with snot,
heaving, the ocean floods my mouth
A little girl shrieks and holds out her arms
asking to be carried away from here
and I have to tell her that there is nowhere, now, to go,
but that splendid things must be coming
that we will go someplace where no one can find us,
 and we will alight there, gently, like gulls.

Self-Portrait as Unknown Woman of the Seine

They will say I am a suicide.
I will still be clothed when I am pulled
from the Seine at Quai de Louvre.
My body will bear no sign of violence.
In the morgue, the pathologist, as he covers
my eyes and mouth with gypsum,
will whisper with his hot wet breath, *très jolie*
and pocket the mold and sell it to a workshop
in Arcueil, where it will be purchased
and copied and photographed.
Before long I will be owned by Rilke.
I will hang in Camus' parlour,
where he will tell his guests
I am the Mona Lisa of the Seine
and sometime later Nabokov
will cast me in a poem as a rusalka,
malevolent spirt of the drowned dead.
Here I ought to say something about how
I think that we all want to die a little sometimes;
we all wish to be found, if not remembered.

A few of these poems have appeared previously, some in different iterations:

"Migraine" – semi-finalist, Nimrod Literary Awards
Pablo Neruda Prize for Poetry

"Self-Portrait as the Unknown Woman of the Seine" – Poet Lore

"On the recovery of Sputnik II, 1957" – The Maine Review

"Elephant" and "Jellyfish" – Cathexis Northwest Press

"Commute" – The Northern Virginia Review

"The Ark on Mt. Ararat" – Little Patuxent Review

"Մայրիկ" – Winner,
Bethesda Urban Partnership Poetry Contest

An abundance of gratitude for those who helped me leave the religion of self-harm:

Ariel, Marissa, & Spencer, my found family;

Gracie, Kendall, Negi, Kat, & Ro, my very best friends;

Max, the brother I did know I needed;

Allison, who holds my hand in the darkness;

Josh, who held my heart;

Jordan, the first and best reader;

David K., who brought me to the pollen path;

My MFA cohort & professors at American University, especially Stephanie, David P., and Kyle;

My friends & professors at George Washington University;

The English department at Ocean City High School;

My friends and pastors at The District Church and The Table Church;

And, above all, my mom, Lu Ann, my dad, Jim, and my sister, Brooke, forever and ever.

Bailey Blumenstock is a poet originally from Ocean City, NJ, though she considers Washington, DC her home. She received her B.A. in Creative Writing and English from The George Washington University, and her MFA in Creative Writing from American University. Presently, she is a student at Wesley Theological Seminary, studying Theology and the Arts. Bailey's work is particularly concerned with her faith, her queerness, and her identity as a diasporic Armenian.

Also Available from Cathexis Northwest Press:

Something To Cry About
by Robert Krantz

Suburban Hermeneutics
by Ian Cappelli

God's Love Is Very Busy
by David Seung

that one time we were almost people
by Christian Czaniecki

Fever Dream/Take Heart
by Valyntina Grenier

The Book of Night & Waking
by Clif Mason

Dead Birds of New Zealand
by Christian Czaniecki

The Weathering of Igneous Rockforms in High-Altitude Riparian Environments
by John Belk

If A Fish
by George Burns

How to Draw a Blank
by Collin Van Son

En Route
by Jesse Wolfe

sky bright psalms
by Temple Cone

Moonbird
by Henry G. Stanton

southern athiest. oh, honey
by d. e. fulford

Bruises, Birthmarks & Other Calamities
by Nadine Klassen

Wanted: Comedy, Addicts
by AR Dugan

They Curve Like Snakes
by David Alexander McFarland

the catalog of daily fears
by Beth Dufford

Shops Close Too Early
by Josh Feit

Vanity Unfair and Other Poems
by Robert Eugene Rubino

Destructive Heresies
by Milo E. Gorgevska

Bodies of Separation
by Chim Sher Ting

The Night with James Dean and Other Prose Poems
by Allison A. deFreese

About Time
by Julie Benesh

Suspended
by Ellen White Rook

The Unempty Spaces Between
by Louis Efron

Quomodo probatur in conflatorio
by Nick Roberts

Suspended
by Ellen White Rook

Call Me Not Ishmael but the Sea
by J. Martin Daughtry

Wild Evolution
by Naomi Leimsider

Coming To Terms
by Peter Sagnella

Acta
by Patrick Wilcox

Honeymoon Shoes
by Valyntina Grenier

Practising Ascending
by Nadine Hitchiner

Home Visit
by Michal Rubin

LA CIUDAD EN TI: THE CITY WITHIN YOU
by Karla Marrufo
Translated from the Spanish by Allison A. deFreese

Resin in the Milky Way
by Amanda Rabaduex

Bone Hunting
by Trinity Catlin

Muskets for the Bear Problem
by Andrew Whitmer

<u>Self-Portraits as a Reddening Sky</u>
by Samuel Gilpin

<u>Desert</u>
by Eric Larsh

<u>Fractured Symphony</u>
by Andi Myles

<u>LA DULZURA DE LOS NAUFRAGIOS: THE SWEETNESS OF SHIPWRECKS</u>
by Karla Marrufo
Translated from the Spanish by Allison A. deFreese

Cathexis Northwest Press

www.ingramcontent.com/pod-product-compliance
Lightning Source LLC
Chambersburg PA
CBHW020443090526
44586CB00045B/830